VALUE STREAM MAPPING

Reduce waste and maximise efficiency

Written by Johann Dumser
Translated by Rebecca Neal

50MINUTES.com

PROPEL
YOUR BUSINESS FORWARD!

PARETO'S PRINCIPLE
Expand your business
with the 80/20 rule

Effort
Result
20%
80%
80%
20%
Important
Not important

Blue Ocean Strategy

Pareto's Principle

Managing Stress at Work

Game Theory

www.50minutes.com

VALUE STREAM MAPPING

- **Names:** value stream mapping (VSM), material and information flow mapping.
- **Uses:** this paper-based diagram includes all the production and management processes, and allows users to take a step back from the current workflow and reorganise it to improve efficiency. It is used in process improvement analysis, process engineering and continuous improvement.
- **Why is it successful?** In some sectors of industry and consulting services, this very thorough mapping tool allows users to visualise and understand the actions undertaken (by the company or an individual) between the moment the customer places an order and the moment they receive the product or service.
- **Key words:**
  - Continuous Improvement: increasing the performance of a company by regularly incorporating small improvements.
  - Kaizen: an approach to quality management through continuous improvement.
  - Lead time: the time it takes to produce or carry out something.
  - Lean management: a kind of management which involves all workers and aims to eliminate waste, sources of inefficiency, performance inhibitors and unnecessary stages in the production process.
  - Lean thinking: a business methodology that aims to provide a new way of thinking. This type of ma-

nagement pushes users to analyse the organisation of human activities to increase profit and empower individuals by eliminating waste.
  ◦ <u>Mapping</u>: the representation of the functioning of an organisation in the form of a diagram.
  ◦ <u>Production value chain</u>: the stages of the production process for a product or service, in chronological order.
  ◦ <u>Pull and push strategies</u>: this means suggesting a product to the customer (push) or giving the customer what they ask for (pull).

Whether a company is going through a period of crisis or growth, it must always have a precise idea of the flow of products and the related communication channels. This reflection should encompass the entire manufacturing process for each product to enable it to optimise efficiency.

Since all businesses, from startups to SMEs to multinationals, aim to maximise profits, more and more managers are adopting the lean approach, which involves systematically eliminating waste in manufacturing processes.

We can all reflect on the way actions are carried out at our level of the company. Although it is important, and even essential, to be able to regularly question ourselves as a matter of course, we need to be aware that it is often not what we do not know that causes the most problems, but rather what we wrongly hold to be true.

Following this logic, departments known as Project Management Offices have been implemented in some large international companies. Their aim is to standardise the language used in the different departments and coordinate projects to encourage continuous improvement. From these combined, constructive synergies, a single methodology emerges: each employee is asked to use clear language that is shared by everyone in all the initiatives launched, with the aim of significantly increasing value for the end client.

In order to remain competitive (meaning to obtain higher quality, lower production costs or a faster production cycle), an organisation will choose between several available techniques. One of these is value stream mapping, which is one of the most successful lean manufacturing tools because it uses a simple diagram to consciously highlight areas for improvement and opportunities.

DEFINITION OF VALUE STREAM MAPPING

Value stream mapping involves representing operations, information flows and data processes in the form of a diagram.

Complementarity of material and information flows

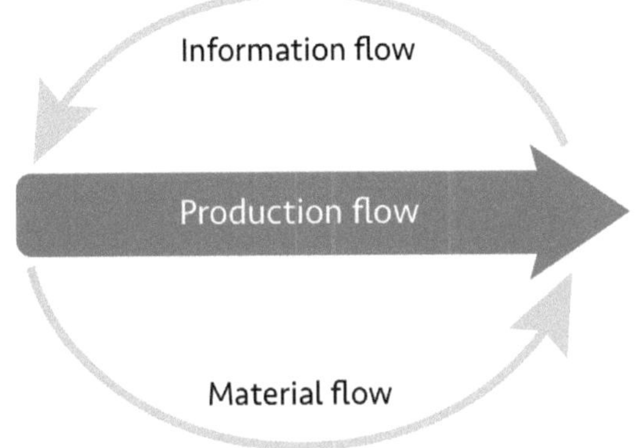

It provides a realistic overview of operations on the ground rather than as they are set out in the company procedures. VSM is always carried out as part of a company's process analysis. The process analysis may be imposed by senior management, an operations manager or a quality manager to increase efficiency, or be offered by service providers (such as an improvement consultant) to reveal previously unidentified opportunities.

In an ideal world, all process modifications would be accompanied by a check, or even a revision if necessary, in order to find out whether a change in the workflow is necessary.

The Japanese engineer and businessman Taiichi Ohno (1912-1990), considered to be the founder of the Toyota Production System, identified seven sources of waste (*muda* in Japanese) in his book *Toyota Production System: Beyond Large-Scale Production* (1988). These have since expanded to eight sources of waste:

- **overproduction**, meaning production carried out earlier, quicker or in larger quantities than the customer asked for;
- **inventory**, which includes reserves of primary materials, pipeline products and finished goods;
- **waiting**, which refers to the waiting time for people or parts over the course of the production cycle;
- **movement**, which means the useless movements of people or material during the manufacturing process (movement of operators);
- **transportation**, which is the useless transport of people or material between manufacturing processes (movement of objects);
- **making defective products**, which includes defective items, flaws, repetitions and corrections in the process;
- **extra processing**, which is processing beyond the level required by the customer;
- **non-utilised talent**, which corresponds to skills that are badly used or not used at all, essentially due to a lack of training or flexibility among the staff.

THEORY

VSM AND VALUE CREATION

In order to understand the concept of VSM, we can begin by outlining its three components: value, stream and mapping.

Value

The value chain was introduced in 1985 by the American professor of business strategy Michael Porter (born in 1947), and aims to create a competitive advantage. It is based on the analysis of a company's internal processes and procedures. In this way, every action in the chain should result in the perception that value has been created (satisfaction) for the final customer, which can be seen in increased turnover for the company. If the term "value" refers to an estimation of the amount customers are prepared to pay to obtain a product or use a service, the actions represents in value stream mapping can be described as "value-adding" or "non-value-adding".

- **Value-adding** steps include all activities which increase the (market or functional) value of the product in the eyes of the customer; in other words, the activities that the customer is prepared to pay for.
- **Non-value-adding** steps are the activities that do not bring any value to the product, which makes them sources of waste. Although all managers aim to get rid of these steps, some of them cannot be avoided (without major investment).

The aim of VSM is to identify processes where little time is spent on value creation in relation to the total amount of time set aside for the work (lead time). It is necessary to define the improvements to apply to the process as a whole in order to increase the proportion of value creation.

Functioning of different improvement methods

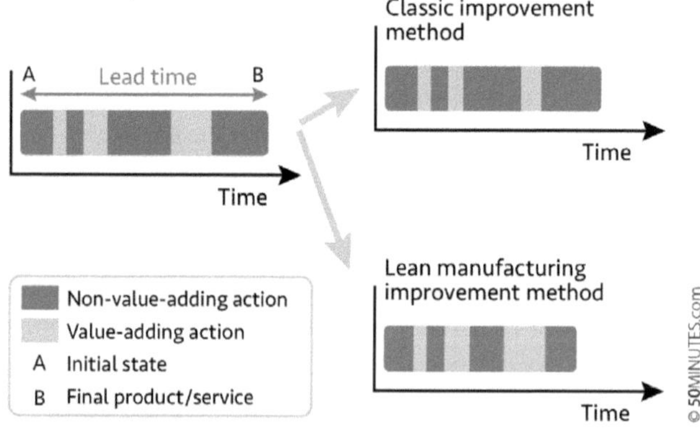

Stream

VSM summarises all the actions in the supply chain of a product or service, taking it from its initial state (A) to the value proposition (B). It is made up of a series of processes set out based on a timeline corresponding to the lead time, meaning the time between the initiation and execution of the process (A-B).

Three categories of processes can be reviewed in VSM:

- **guiding processes** (management, strategy, quality control, environment, safety, finance, and so on);
- **operational processes** (manufacturing, design, development, shipping, and so on);
- **support processes** (purchasing, human resources, and so on).

Mapping

Mapping is a clear, simple way of representing the functioning of a business (in the manufacture of a product or the development of a service) visually. This tool aims to work on a whole rather than just on an isolated part. This means that the analysis focuses not on the level of a machine within a production line, but on the level of the production line as a whole.

The map must always be ordered using icons and must follow given standards to make it understandable to everyone involved. It is organised based on three main types of action:

- information flow,
- material flow,
- figures.

Zones used in value stream mapping

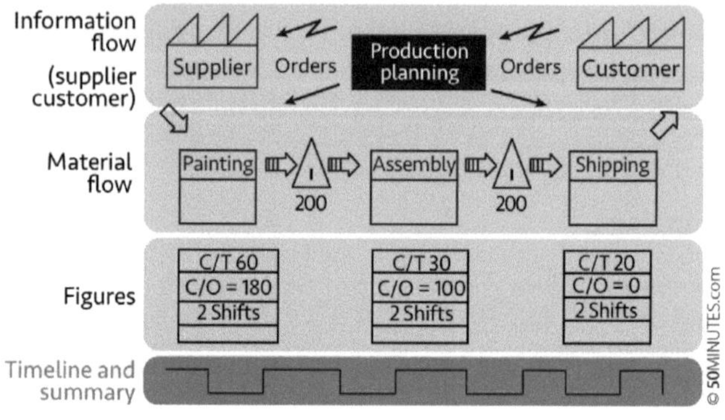

WHERE DO I START?

The method involves the following steps:

- following the production process of a product, starting with the customer (a need) and continuing to the supplier;
- representing each action in the material and information flow visually;
- reflecting on key points and drawing up the future value chain.

Chain of value creation for a product

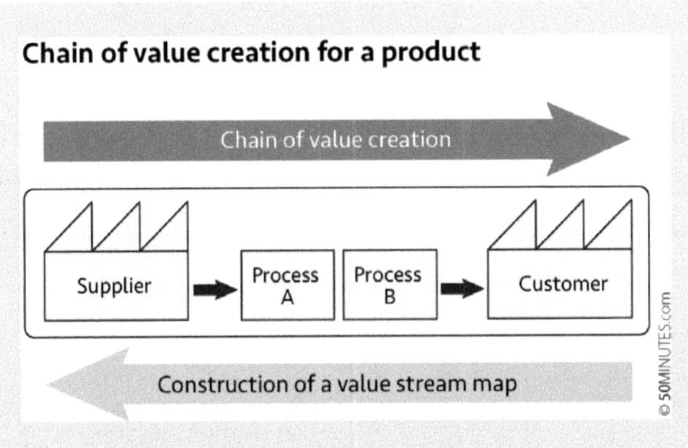

VSM AND ITS ICONS

The main symbols used in VSM

Process symbols		
Icon	**Name**	**Description**
	Customer/ supplier	External source corresponding to a supplier (placed top left) or a customer (placed top right)
	Process	Process with an operator (currently in place) which can add value to the product (the name of the process is normally placed in the top box, while the function is described in the centre)
	Data box	Space for figures placed below other icons which contains information needed to analyse the system (processing time, lead time, changeover time, and so on)

<table>
<tr><td colspan="3" align="center">Information symbols</td></tr>
<tr><td align="center">Icon</td><td align="center">Name</td><td align="center">Description</td></tr>
<tr><td></td><td>Production Kanban</td><td>Trigger of the production of a given number of pieces</td></tr>
<tr><td></td><td>Batch Kanban</td><td>Batch</td></tr>
<tr><td></td><td>Database</td><td>Database</td></tr>
<tr><td>Information</td><td>Information</td><td>Text box including additional information</td></tr>
</table>

<table>
<tr><th colspan="3">Material symbols</th></tr>
<tr><th>Icon</th><th>Name</th><th>Description</th></tr>
<tr><td></td><td>Physical pull</td><td>Physical removal of material from a supermarket</td></tr>
<tr><td></td><td>Truck shipment</td><td>Delivery using external transport services from a supplier (possible to add information about the frequency of delivery in an information box under the icon)</td></tr>
<tr><td></td><td>Inventory</td><td>Stock of raw materials or finished products (possible to add information about the time period under the icon)</td></tr>
<tr><td></td><td>Supermarket</td><td>Supermarket stock containing the available inventories for the downstream flow (the customer can use it when necessary); the following process carries out a pull of this inventory</td></tr>
<tr><td></td><td>Push arrow</td><td>Push arrow of information or material from one process to another; a process produces a good independently of needs downstream</td></tr>
</table>

Material symbols		
Icon	**Name**	**Description**
┅┅┅┅┅▶	Pull arrow	Pull arrow which indicates a pull removal (reduction in stock which has no impact on operations upstream) on the previous processes
──FIFO──▶	FIFO flow	First in, first out principle (the first to enter is the first to leave)
	Operator	Operator associated with a process; indicates the completion of all or part of the actions of a process
OXOX	Load levelling	Means used to intercept batches of Kanban cards and level their volume over a given time period
	Phone	Information received by telephone
	Kaizen burst	Need to improve a specific point of the process which is critical to complete the mapping of the future state
──────▶	Manual info flow	Manual information flow
	Electronic info flow	Electronic information flow (internet, intranet, exchange of electronic data, and so on)

Material symbols		
Icon	**Name**	**Description**
	Safety stock	Stock reserved in case of special circumstances
	Shipment	Product flow from a supplier to a process or from a process to a customer
	Signal Kanban	Warning indicating that the supermarket inventory between two processes has gone down to a trigger threshold or below a given previously established minimum level
	Timeline segment	Value-adding time (processing times) or non-value-adding time (wait times)
	Timeline total	End of the lead time and summary of all the value-adding and non-value-adding time
	Delay	Delay or time constraint
	Rework	Iterations or need to rework

VSM AND ITS ADVANTAGES

There are several advantages to using VSM, as the tool:

- offers a simple, cross-sectional overview of the entire process;

- incorporates all the information needed to visually understand the two types of flow (information and material);
- identifies the signs and causes of waste;
- coordinates the language used to discuss the process thanks to standardised icons and rules, which makes teamwork easier (analysis, identification of areas for improvement, putting across ideas, and so on).

More broadly, value stream mapping supports the demonstration of value creation and problem solving. It establishes efficient, consistent and cross-sectional dialogue between the different departments of a company and encourages the development of a culture of perfection.

PRACTICAL APPLICATION

BEST PRACTICES – STEPS

VSM is part of a DMAIC (Define, Measure, Analyse, Improve, Control) approach, because drawing up a map is not an end in itself: it is only the first stage in a classic improvement study of a value chain.

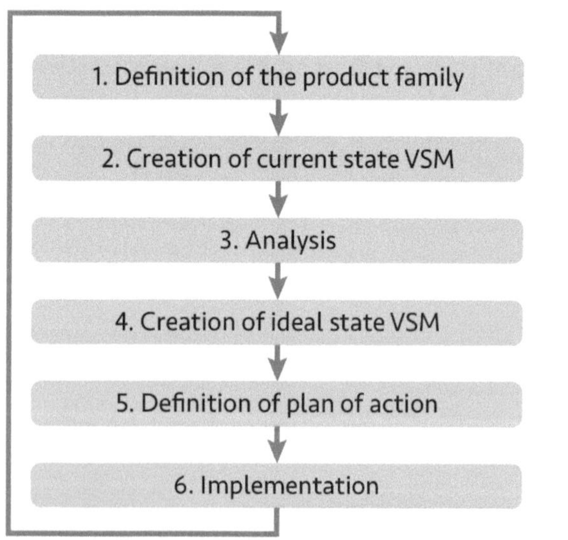

Step 1: Definition of the product family

Before carrying out value stream mapping, you need to choose a family of products to analyse. Since your approach's chances of success depend on this choice, you should pay plenty of attention to it.

To halt an area of work, you need to be aware of possible current problems and their impact. For example, you could use a Pareto chart (a chart which represents the importance of the different causes of a phenomenon; the goal here is to outline a working zone to carry out VSM) or ask the managers of different departments (such as the head of production or the director). The main questions you should ask yourself are:

- How much turnover does this product family represent?
- What are the losses caused by these products?
- What are the chances of success of value stream mapping? (Do not choose an area that is too difficult or too simple; do not tackle the analysis of all the production in your company or, conversely, the analysis of a single, overly simple department.)
- What is the production strategy?

N.B.

Do not be surprised if you are asked to study the processes of a product family which generates little revenue. This may turn out to be a smart move if it is responsible for heavy losses.

Step 2: Creation of the current state VSM

In order to create a new, improved version of the map of the value chain of a product family, the first thing you will need to do is to get a precise idea of the current situation and map it. How do things work now? Who does what? How much time does it take? How do the different services communicate with one another? What are the responsibilities and specific features of each position in the chain? The different stages in drawing up the map are discussed in detail below. The aim here is to take stock of the material and information flows, try to understand the current functioning of the workshop or department, calculate the lead time and understand the sources and causes of waste.

- **Phase zero: preparation**
  - Start by observing the activities of the factory or service.
  - Collect precise, up-to-date information on behalf of the person who wants this VSM. If necessary, take measurements on the ground with the help of a timer by working your way around the circuit of raw materials and information.
  - Start your itinerary with the customer and work your way back through the manufacturing process. Make a list of the processes that are most closely linked to the final customer in order to identify what is absolutely useful to them.
  - Sketch a draft by hand on a single side of A3 or A4 paper.
- **First phase: the customer**
  - Write "customer" in the top right-hand corner.
- **Second phase: the manufacturing process**
  - Use the "process" icon (the material undergoing operations) and:

* group the positions belonging to a single process under the same icon;
    * include the important information about the process in the box below (such as the cycle time, value-adding time, time period, manufacturing change time, number of each piece per hour, available working time, and so on).
  ◦ Use the "stock" icon.
- **Third phase: the supplier**
  ◦ Write "supplier" in the top left-hand corner.
  ◦ Indicate the frequency and mode of delivery (as information next to the supplier):
    * a large arrow indicates a primary delivery between two factories;
    * a lorry (or a boat, a plane, and so on) indicates the mode of delivery.
- **Fourth phase: information**
  ◦ Draw a straight line for physical information flows (for example by mail) or a zigzag line for electronic information flows.
  ◦ Indicate the frequency (of sending or transmission) in a box at the side.
  ◦ Specify the mode (internet, paper, and so on):
    * the push mode, which is based on the forecast of needs for the process downstream, often results in intermediary stocks between processes;
    * the pull mode, which represents a production demand from the downstream process to the upstream process, reduces the number of items in production.

- **Fifth phase: the timeline**
  - Draw the line under the manufacturing process boxes and stock icons to calculate the lead time, meaning all the time taken for each stage (corresponding to the processing time) and the storage time.
- **Sixth phase: mapping of the value chain complete**
  - Once the map of the current situation is complete, start analysing and observing areas of waste and outlining possible improvements to create the VSM of the future state you are aiming for.

Step 3: Analysis

Once you have finished this stage, the next thing to do is to analyse and observe the material and information flows in detail in order to determine what is working efficiently and what is not working so well. This stage is particularly crucial, as it allows you to identify waste and areas for improvement. Make sure that you get the right people involved: whether they are the heads of services, participants in the process or project managers who will oversee the transition, they must be open to improvements and change.

This exercise must be well-prepared and well-presented in order to avoid rushing the people whose work features in the VSM. The aim here is to show them that it is possible to make their work more profitable and create more value for the customer, whether they are internal or external. As a general rule, simply taking into account the main improvement factors below will have an impact on the final result:

- just-in-time manufacturing;
- general implementation of a continuous flow wherever possible, with the aim of reducing or even eliminating stocks, or insertion of supermarkets (intermediary stocks managed by Kanban batches);
- grouping all the information on the customer order into a single process (known as the "pacemaker process") which guides the other processes.

Step 4: Creation of ideal state VSM

Armed with your observations and the measures you have planned, this step will allow you to draw up a map detailing the opportunities for improvement identified earlier. The final aim of the ideal state VSM is to reduce the non-value-adding time so that the total time is as close as possible to the value-adding time. In general, it takes around three to five working days to draw up the current state and ideal state VSM.

Step 5: Definition of plan of action

For each change, the team in charge of the project will organise a plan of action. It will be important to quantify the associated benefits and solutions (costs/resources) to convince senior management of the actions envisaged and ensure that they are approved. Implementing a plan of action can take several months or even several years.

Step 6: Implementation

Once the budget has been approved, risk management has been carried out and the organisation has been stopped, it is time to put the plan into action. This includes development, acceptance, employee training and change management.

RECOMMENDATIONS

There are two major areas to pay particular attention to: the organisation of the team and the methodology.

Organisational warnings	Methodological warnings

• Organise a multidisciplinary project team: six to eight people will be enough. For an efficient group dynamic, opt for a 1/3, 1/3, 1/3 split, as described below:
  o 1/3 users (people who know the subject);
  o 1/3 customers (internal or external, but who can perceive the added value);
  o 1/3 "fresh eyes" (project manager, other departments, managers).
• Do not do this exercise alone without input from other people. Operational staff absolutely must be involved. This should not just come from above: you must explain it and see that operators participate.
• Avoid only letting external consultants work on the project; instead, seize the opportunity to develop the skills of internal staff. There are individual development (training) programmes focused on lean methods, which are a way of investing in your staff. It is up to managers and human resources staff to convince senior management of the value of lean thinking (which increases employees' active participation in analysis, detection and the maintenance of good processes, and is part of a process of continuous improvement).
	• Pay attention to your priorities! For example, make sure that you select the right product family for your exercise.
	• Do not do everything at once. Choose one area as a kind of test and use the results to drive progress in your most important area.
	• Draw up the map of ideal stages. Be bold and include all your opportunities, and then select the ones you are going to work on to start with.
	• Simplify your mapping so that you only retain what is essential.
	• Periodically revise your mapping.

If the VSM is poorly understood, it will result in lost time.

CASE STUDY

We are going to focus on the current state VSM of the fictional company Forest LPC, which makes furniture. The product family we are studying for this exercise is stools.

First phase: the customer

* The customer is placed in the top right-hand corner.

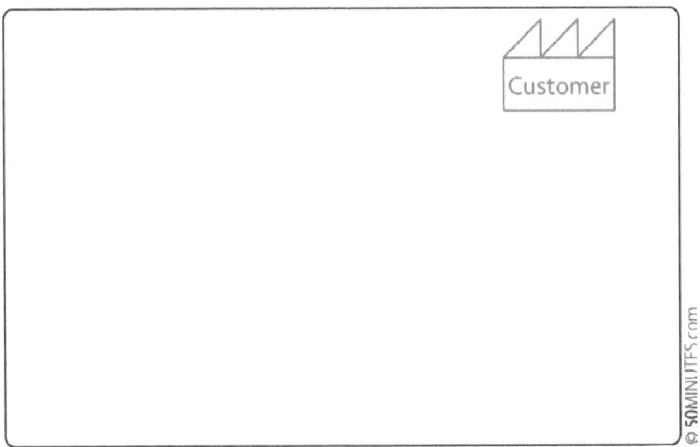

Second phase: The manufacturing process

* This stage comprises four processes: painting, assembly, packaging and shipping.
* Alongside each process are the workstations and important information (cycle time, changeover time or

alterations to a machine to produce another product, shifts, and so on).

- The intermediary stocks at each stage are also filled in.

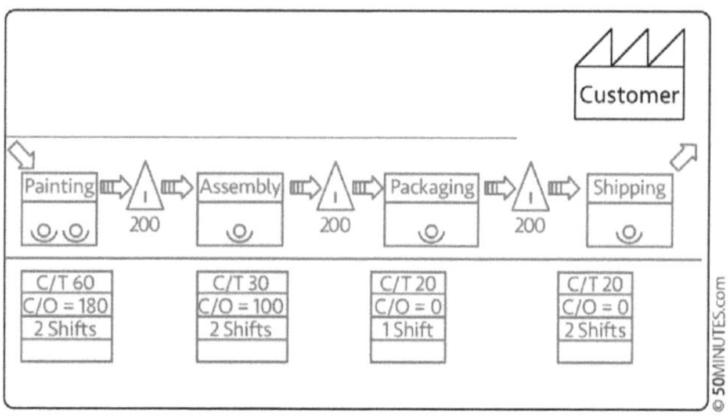

Third phase: The supplier

- The supplier is indicated in the top left-hand corner.
- The weekly delivery is carried out by lorry.

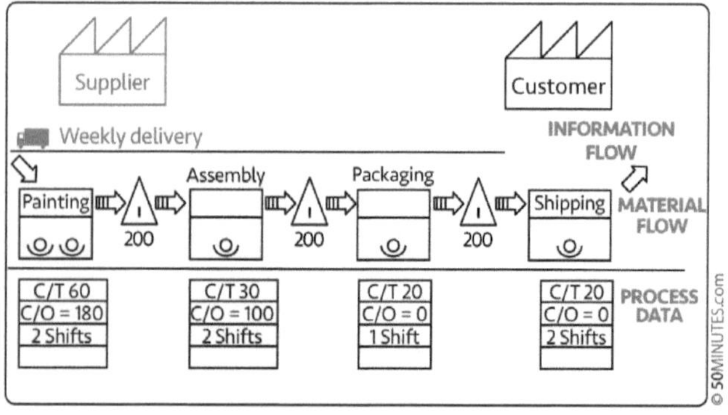

Fourth phase: Information

- Weekly demand forecasts are sent by the customer to the company via email.
- Orders are passed on to the supplier by fax.
- A weekly schedule is given to each internal position within the company.
- Information and physical (or material) flows are then clearly represented.

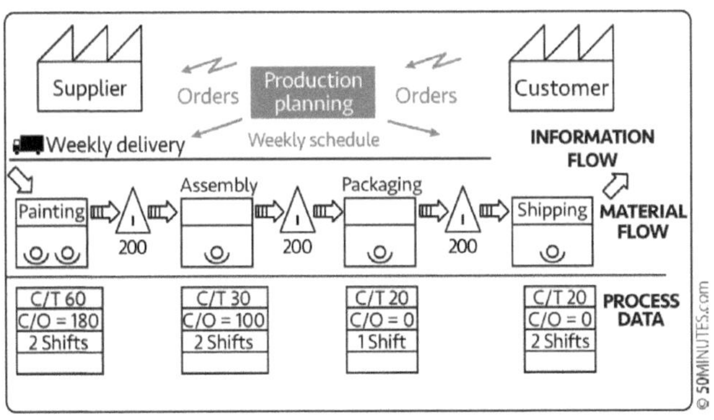

Fifth phase: The timeline

- A timeline is added underneath the manufacturing process boxes and stock icons.
- The process has a lead time of 19 days and a processing time of 365 seconds.

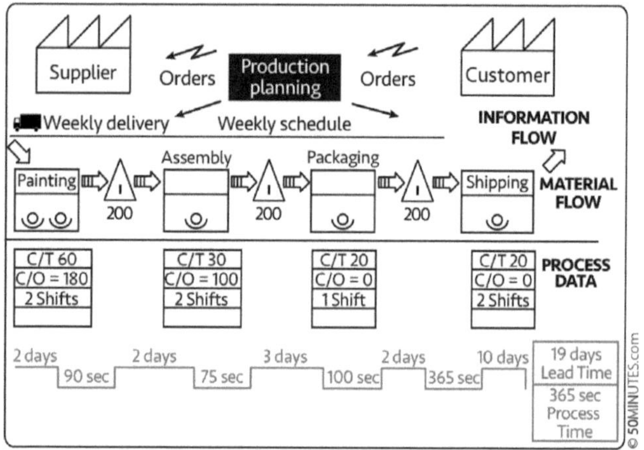

Sixth phase: VSM complete

The mapping of the current situation is therefore finished. It is now time to analyse it, observe areas of waste and identify possible improvements. We can list the following sources of improvement by including them on the diagram, which will allow us to prepare the map of the target situation:

- basing planning on weekly customer orders instead of forecasts;
- creating a pull system for production planning;
- creating a supermarket just before the start of painting;
- eliminating rejections from painting;
- combining the packaging and shipping processes.

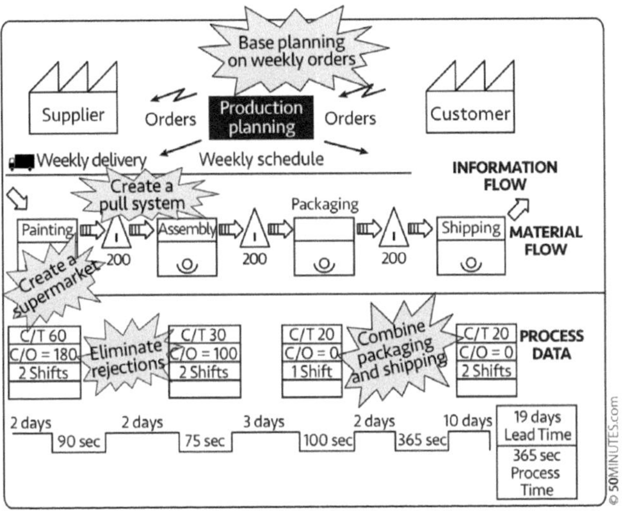

Base planning on weekly orders
Supplier
Orders
Production planning
Orders
Customer
Weekly delivery
Weekly schedule
INFORMATION FLOW
Create a pull system
Packaging
Painting
Assembly
200
200
Shipping
MATERIAL FLOW
200
Create a supermarket
C/T 60
C/O = 180
2 Shifts
Eliminate rejections
C/T 30
C/O = 100
2 Shifts
C/T 20
C/O = 0
1 Shift
Combine packaging and shipping
C/T 20
C/O = 0
2 Shifts
PROCESS DATA
2 days
2 days
3 days
2 days
10 days
19 days Lead Time
90 sec
75 sec
100 sec
365 sec
365 sec Process Time
© 50MINUTES.com

IMPACT

LIMITATIONS AND CRITICISMS

As well as its many advantages, value stream mapping has some limitations.

- **Possible mistakes when drawing up the map.**
  - Errors can creep in due to incorrect gathering, transcription or analysis of the data. To avoid this, use experts who can look at the situation objectively and multidisciplinary teams.
  - Always pay attention to what you are analysing, because some processes do not need to be revised.
- **It is only a tool.** Value stream mapping is not an end in itself; it reveals problems in the company, helps users to reflect and, above all, should lead to action.
  There is no point analysing if you do not put a plan of action in place! Make sure you do not get bogged down in the analysis phase. Furthermore, if different groups are working on lean projects, you should take care to coordinate them well to get the best out of all the projects.
- **Neglect of the human and social aspects.** VSM is a technical tool which only deals with the physical aspects, interactions and the guiding of flows. It does not incorporate the social, human and organisational dimensions, which are nonetheless very important in a lean project. This tendency is even more marked in the industrial sector, where managers are very focused on the technical side of things but are less inclined to think about human issues.

- **Restrictive use of standardised symbols.** The existing symbols can hold back the search for innovative solutions. However, innovation is increasingly necessary for companies that are trying to remain competitive.

RELATED MODELS AND EXTENSIONS

DMAIC

The DMAIC (Define, Measure, Analyse, Improve, Control) model is a structured approach which allows users to resolve problems. It provides the continuous improvement team with a five-step base to work from. In this powerful lean project management method, the define stage is key.

- Define: identification of the object of study and description of the objective of the work to be carried out by the team.
- Measure: gathering of information to complete the map of the processes and definition of the performance indicators to monitor the project effectively.
- Analyse: identification of the causes of problems and analysis of their sources.
- Improve: suggestion of solutions, planning of actions, implementation of the chosen measures.
- Control: comparison of the expected effects and results obtained after the implementation of solutions, communication on the project, review to draw conclusions.

Lean manufacturing

This well-known method for eliminating waste requires some collective intelligence for convincing results: the teams working on this lean project must be motivated, coordinated and determined to find solutions. The five key elements are:

- the definition of added value from the customer's point of view;
- the identification of the value chain with regard to the different stages of production;
- particular attention to the flows, making sure that the value-adding stages are not stopped;
- pull flows, prioritising customer orders rather than forecasts;
- perfection by setting ambitious goals and introducing a dynamic of continuous improvement.

Kaizen

Kaizen is Japanese for "continuous improvement", and is based on small improvements introduced on a daily basis, with all the people involved in the process participating and making the necessary effort.

Kaizen does not immediately lead to spectacular results because it is introduced slowly, but it often proves much more effective over the long term. It can be contrasted with innovation, which requires major investment and involves sudden change.

SIPOC

This modelling tool involves drawing up a general table of the macro functioning of a given process. The SIPOC (Suppliers, Inputs, Process, Outputs, Customers) diagram allows users to define the limits of the macro process, summarise the inputs and outputs and identify the suppliers and customers. But watch out: it only represents material flows.

SUMMARY

- VSM is the key tool of lean manufacturing. It aims to detect sources of waste in the value chain for a given product family.
- Today, VSM is used in all domains of industry because it responds to the universal and growing need to reduce production costs.
- It is a good idea to begin a lean transformation with value stream mapping. You need to know not only the different stages, but also the best practices to ensure a clear overview of the procedures that make up a company.
- Current state and ideal state VSM are part of a continuous improvement method. This method is used not only to describe the current situation, but also to imagine and establish a more efficient, more responsive, less costly and more coordinated future situation. The diagram of information and material flows allows users to tackle two issues at once: waste reduction and the improvement of working conditions.
- The context of the organisation around the project is essential to ensure its success. Multidisciplinary teams, including people as close to the ground as possible, and the firm commitment of senior management are key factors in this approach to change.
- Finally, it is also important to be aware of the limitations of this method. In particular, VSM does not focus on the analysis of social, psychological and organisational aspects.
- VSM is one of the most widely used methods thanks to its

ease of use and effectiveness at inspiring users to reflect.

We want to hear from you!
Leave a comment on your online library
and share your favourite books on social media!

FURTHER READING

BIBLIOGRAPHY

- Davis, J. (2006) *Lean Manufacturing.* New York: Industrial Press.
- Fouque, F. (2009) *À la découverte du Lean Six Sigma.* Mions: Édition Fouque.
- Hohmann, C. (2009) *Techniques de productivité. Comment gagner des points de performance pour les managers et les encadrants.* Paris: Éditions Eyrolles.
- Hohmann, C. (No date) Lean Enterprise. *Christian. Hohmann.fr.* [Online]. [Accessed 26 July 2017]. Available from: <http://christian.hohmann.free.fr/index.php/lean-entreprise>
- Lean Enterprise Institute. (No date) What is Lean? *Lean.org.* [Online]. [Accessed 26 July 2017]. Available from: <https://www.lean.org/whatslean/>
- Ohno, T. (1988) *Toyota Production System: Beyond Large-Scale Production.* New York: Productivity Press.
- Porter, M. E. (1985) *Competitive Advantage: Creating and Sustaining Superior Performance.* New York: Free Press.
- Rother, M. and Shook, J. (1999) *Learning to See.* New York: Productivity Press.
- Subramaniam, A. (2010) VSM – Current & Future: How to maximise the overall flow? *SlideShare.* [Online]. [Accessed 26 July 2017]. Available from: <https://fr.slideshare.net/anandsubramaniam/vsm-current-future>
- Womack, J. P. and Jones, J. T. (1996) *Lean Thinking.* New York: Free Press.

ADDITIONAL SOURCES

- Conceptdraw website: http://conceptdraw.com/samples/quality-VSM
- Marris Consulting website: http://www.marris-consulting.com/
- Strategos website: http://www.strategosinc.com/

VIDEO

- The Karen Martin Group. (2014) *Value Stream Mapping: Case Studies*. [Online]. [Accessed 26 July 2017]. Available from: <https://www.youtube.com/watch?v=ZPNq5k24vgY&feature=youtu.be>

50MINUTES.com
History
Business
Coaching
Book Review
Health & Wellbeing